21-Day Clean-Eating Meal Plan - 1200-1500 Calories

Healthy Recipes: The 3-Week Weight Loss Cookbook for Beginners. Part 2

By Karla Bro

Disclaimer

All material in "21-Day Clean-Eating Meal Plan – 1200-1500 Calories. Healthy Recipes: The 3-Week Weight Loss Cookbook for Beginners. Part 2" is provided for your information only and may not be construed as medical advice or instruction. No action or inaction should be taken based solely on the contents of this information. Consult appropriate professionals for your health and well-being.

Remember that cooking is subjective. You may not achieve the results desired due to different brands of ingredients or different cooking abilities. Make sure you are not allergic to any ingredients.

I am not a chef. I'm just a person who likes cooking and writing about home-cooked food. Most of my recipes are created based on personal taste.

Table of Contents

Introduction

Hello, reader!

Today, clean nutrition is interpreted differently. Still, after consulting with a certified nutritionist, I settled on an option that provided for a balance in proteins, fats, and carbohydrates. And it's better to be guided by the following principles for clean eating diet:

- To eat foods most naturally and cooked gently, only raw, boiled, stewed or baked.
- Canned food and processed foods are taboo: for example, replace white flour with whole grain.
- Choose the daily norm of 1200-1600 calories.
- Refused sugar and sugary food, which contains trans fats and preservatives, as well as processed food. Replace sugar with honey.
- Try to abandon the dishes with many ingredients and ensure the cooking time of most dishes did not exceed one hour.
- Try to introduce only seasonal vegetables and fruits.
- Begin eating five meals a day, and the first meal was supposed to take place within two hours after waking up. Subsequent meals were eaten at intervals of 2.5 to 3.5 hours.
- Drink water at least 7 glasses per day.

Clean Eating Rules

Shopping

First, go to the grocery store and pay attention to the signs in the produce section about how far your fruits, veggies, meat, and fish had to travel to reach you. Read nutrition labels, and don't choose products with unknown ingredients. Instead, try to pick foods without boxes, cans, bags, and packaging. All the food must be fresh.

Cooking

Cook at home, and you will know all about salt and sugar in your meal. Don't use high-fat cooking methods, such as deep-frying or stewing with animal or vegetable fat. You can steam, bake, or grill. Use olive oil, replace salt with garlic, spices, herbs, and lemon.

Whole Grains and Natural Sugars

Try to complete your meal with whole grains for your clean eating meal plan. Choose legumes and beans. They will be useful for your heart. Natural sugar must be in your meal plan. Use honey, maple sugar, or dehydrated sugar cane juice. There is no fat, cholesterol in the organic sweeteners.

You can eat the following:

- Single-ingredient grains (farro, oats, barley, brown rice, quinoa, millet, and amaranth)
- Whole-wheat pasta
- Popcorn
- Sprouted whole-grain bread
- Whole-wheat pizza dough

Protein

Don't forget about protein, a vital muscle-builder. It's essential in the first part of the day. Make sure to eat proteins at breakfast and lunch. Clean proteins are these:

- Chicken breasts and legs, ground beef
- Seafood, such as wild salmon and Pacific cod
- Eggs
- Unflavored nuts, such as almonds, hazelnuts, cashews, and walnuts
- Plain nut butter without sugar
- Dried beans

Fruits and Vegetables

These products are always a clear choice. Don't worry about sugar content. It's hard to overdo it. Tasty fruits and useful vegetables contain a lot of fiber, vitamins, and minerals.

It's better to limit your consumption of fruit juice because even 100% fruit juice doesn't contain the beneficial fiber of the whole fruits.

It's better to choose these:

- Fresh fruit
- Canned fruit without sugar
- Frozen fruit without sugar
- Dried fruit without sugar

Vegetables are the building blocks of clean-eating meals. They contain a lot of vitamins, minerals, and fiber. Canned and frozen vegetables are healthy too, but choose ones without sauces and read the labels.

Choose these vegetables:

- Any fresh vegetables
- Frozen and canned vegetables without sauce or salt.

Dairy

It's better to choose nondairy alternatives than dairy products. Choices are coconut, soy, and almond milk. If you like dairy products, use regular or Greek yogurt, choose unsweetened varieties and low-fat products. Whole-milk dairy is the best choice.

Choose the following:

- Plain yogurt
- Milk
- Cheese
- Unsweetened nondairy milk

How to Transitions to a Clean Diet

1. The decision should be well thought out and not just emotional. So, determine the reason and tell yourself, "That's why I turned to clean food, and I am not going to turn off my intended path!"

2. Allocate time. Sit down and think about how much time you can devote to a new lifestyle. You may have to spend an extra hour a day preparing a healthy lunch.

3. Goals should be measurable and straightforward. If you love cookies, telling yourself, "I will eat fewer cookies" is abstract. While saying, "I will eat one cookie a day" is more specific, it is better to say, "Instead of cookies, I will eat fruit."

4. Get rid of harmful products. List all your favorite "harmful" products. You need to throw away artificial, ultra-processed foods from your refrigerator and pantry.

5. Replenish your stocks with "clean" products. Gradually replace harmful products with clean products. Start with fruits and vegetables. Then include wholegrain food in your diet.

6. Start your day with a fresh breakfast. Fruit and green smoothies are a good option. Eat this way for 1-2 weeks, and you'll develop the desire to eat clean lunches and dinners.

7. Do not eat when you are full. Do you not know proper portions? Then, stop eating when your stomach is full.

8. Study labels and choose products with natural ingredients.

9. Get to know your local farmers. They will be able to supply you with independently grown, organic products.

10. Start cooking.

11. Adhere to the clean food plan.

Count the Calories

If you want to lose weight, reduce your number of calories, and increase your physical activity. If you wish to lose 1 to 1 ½ pound per week, reduce your calorie intake by 500-750 calories:

A diet with 1200 to 1500 calories per day is safe for women;

A food with 1500 to 1800 calories per day is safe for men and women who exercise regularly.

Don't use low-calorie diets of fewer than 800 calories per day. You can only eat in this way if your doctor is monitoring you.

We made the meal plan for 21 days and used a 1200-1600 calorie diet menu. You can combine meals and ingredients to taste and complement the list for the day. Also, increase portions if you want to cook for the whole family.

We recommend this menu for 1 to 6 people and use "1200-1500 calories a day meal plan".

DAY 1 (1295 calories)

Breakfast

White Cabbage Salad with Carrots, 5 oz

Snack 1

A cup of tea,

1 oz Parmesan cheese,

2 tsp honey

Lunch

Braised Chicken, 7 oz

Fresh cucumbers, 7 oz

Snack 2

1 oz pumpkin seeds

1/2 apple

Dinner

Braised Chicken, 9 oz

2 pieces whole-grain toast, 2 oz

Broccoli Wok with Garlic, 5 oz

White Cabbage Salad with Carrots

(2 servings)

Ingredients

7 oz white cabbage
3 ½ oz carrots
2 oz onions
2 tbsp olive oil
Salt and pepper to taste

Directions

1. Wash and peel the carrots.
2. Wash the cabbage.
3. Chop vegetables.
4. Cut onion into thin half-rings.

5. Place the vegetables in a medium bowl. Add salt, pepper, and olive oil. Stir the ingredients.

Nutritional facts per serving: 144.55 calories, 2.8g protein, 10.13g fat, 10.75 g carbs

Braised Chicken

(2 servings)

Ingredients

1 1/8 lb chicken breast

1/4 cup water

Salt to taste

Directions

1. Wash the chicken.
2. In a thick-bottom stewpan, add chicken breast and water. Cover the pan tightly.
3. Stew for 30 minutes. Salt to taste. Stew for another 30 minutes.

Nutritional facts per serving: 225 calories, 57.75g protein, 3g fat

Broccoli Wok with Garlic

(4 servings)

Ingredients

1 1/3 lb broccoli

3 cloves garlic

2 tbsp olive or corn oil

Directions

1. Wash the broccoli. Cut it.
2. Boil 2 liters of water in a saucepan. Add broccoli to boiling water.
3. Boil for 5-7 minutes. Drain the water.
4. Preheat a pan and add oil. Once the oil is hot, add the broccoli.
5. Cook for 5 minutes. Add the cloves of garlic and salt.
6. Cook for 15-20 minutes.

Nutritional facts per serving: 77.75 calories, 4.6g protein, 3.5g fat, 8.6g carbs

DAY 2 (1184 calories)

Breakfast
Omelet with Vegetables and Linseed Flour
Carrot, Apple and Orange Salad, 4 oz

Snack 1
1 oz of gouda cheese,
2 tsp honey and a cup of black tea

Lunch
Broccoli, Cauliflower and Zucchini Cream Soup, 10 oz

Snack 2
1 oz peanuts
Carrot, Apple and Orange Salad, 4 oz

Dinner
Chicken Gizzards with Zucchini and Leek, 10 oz

Omelet with Vegetables and Linseed Flour

(2 servings)

Ingredients
4 eggs
1/2 bell pepper
1 oz onion
2 oz zucchini
1 tbsp corn oil
2 tbsp sour cream
1 tbsp linseed flour

Directions

1. Wash and peel the vegetables. Finely chop the onion. Dice the pepper and zucchini.

2. Heat corn oil in a non-stick pan. Place the plants in the pan and fry, stirring for 5 minutes, until softened.

3. Break the eggs into a medium bowl.

4. Add sour cream to the eggs and beat well.

5. Add linseed flour to the egg mixture. Beat well.

6. Pour the mixture into a pan with the vegetables. Cover and cook for 10 minutes over low heat. Flip the omelet. Cook another 2-3 minutes.

Nutritional facts per serving: 304 calories, 15.5g protein, 24.03g fat, 5g carbs

Carrot, Apple and Orange Salad

(2 servings)

Ingredients

3 ½ oz carrots
3 ½ oz apples
2 oz orange
2 tbsp yogurt
1 tsp honey

Directions

1. Wash and peel the carrots. Grate finely.
2. Cut the apple into small slices.
3. Peel the orange, separate the lobes. Chop finely.
4. Stir all the ingredients in a medium bowl.
5. Mix yogurt and honey. Add the mixture to the main ingredients.

Nutritional facts per serving: 75.3 calories, 1.97g protein, 0.7g fat, 15.28g carbs

Broccoli, Cauliflower and Zucchini Cream Soup

(4 servings)

Ingredients

1 lb 1 ½ oz broccoli
1 lb 1 ½ oz cauliflower
10 oz zucchini
1/2 cup milk
2 L water
1 ½ oz gouda cheese
Salt to taste
1 medium onion
1 tsp corn oil (or olive)

Directions

1. Pour water and milk into the pan.

2. Wash and cut vegetables. Separate the broccoli and cauliflower florets.

3. Put the vegetables into the milk-water mixture. Cook over medium heat for 30 minutes.

4. Peel and finely chop the onion. Add corn oil to a non-stick pan and heat. Add onion and simmer for 5-7 minutes, stirring constantly.

5. Remove the pan from the heat. Add onions to the pan. In a blender, beat vegetables into the broth.

6. Grate the cheese and add to the soup. Return the pan to the heat. Stir over low heat for 10-15 minutes.

Nutritional facts per serving: 173.54 calories, 12.3g protein, 7.27g fat, 19.2g carbs

Chicken Gizzards with Zucchini and Leek

(4 servings)

Ingredients

1 lb 1 ½ oz chicken gizzards

3 ½ oz leeks

1 lb 1 ½ oz zucchini

1 tbsp olive oil

Salt to taste

Directions

1. Wash and cut the chicken gizzards.
2. Wash the zucchini and cut into thin slices.
3. Wash the leek and chop finely.
4. Mix gizzards and vegetable ingredients. Add salt to taste.

5. Grease the baking sheet with oil. Put the mixture on the baking sheet in a single layer.

6. Preheat the oven to 350 °F.

7. Bake for 40-50 minutes.

Nutritional facts per serving: 193.2 calories, 25.12g protein, 7.9g fat, 6.55g carbs

DAY 3 (1401 calories)

Breakfast

Omelet with Vegetables and Linseed Flour(same as Day 2)

Snack 1

Banana-Oatmeal Cookies with Cottage Cheese, 2 cookies (2 oz)

Lunch

Broccoli, Cauliflower and Zucchini Cream Soup, 10 oz (same as Day 2)

2 whole-grain bread toasts, 2 oz

Snack 2

Banana-Oatmeal Cookies with Cottage Cheese, 2 cookies (2 oz)
1 cup of milk

Dinner

Chicken Gizzards with Zucchini and Leek, 10 oz
Buckwheat Porridge, 3 ½ oz

Banana-Oatmeal Cookies with Cottage Cheese

(12 servings)

Ingredients
5 oz oatmeal
7 oz cottage cheese
5 oz banana
2 tsp honey

Directions

1. Preheat the oven. Bake cookies for 30-40 minutes at 350 ^{0}F.
2. Peel the bananas and place them in a large bowl. Mash with a fork.
3. Add oatmeal.
4. Mix ingredients well.
5. Pour honey into the mixture and mix again.

6. Linea baking sheet with the parchment paper.

7. Form 12-14 balls from the mixture. Put them on parchment paper and flatten slightly.

Nutritional facts per serving: 325.86 calories, 6.7g protein, 3.47g fat, 12.3g carbs

Buckwheat Porridge

(6 servings)

Ingredients
7 oz buckwheat
1 1/2 liters of water
1 oz corn oil
Salt to taste

Directions
1. Rinse the buckwheat groats.
2. Boil water in a saucepan. Add the grain.
3. Cook for 10 minutes. Add oil and salt.
4. Cook until porridge until thickens.

Nutritional facts per serving: 134.3 calories, 4.2g protein, 4.43g fats, 20.7g carbs

DAY 4 (1383 calories)

Breakfast

Grilled chicken cutlet, 3 ½ oz
Beetroot Salad, 5 oz

Snack 1

Two Banana-Oatmeal Cookies with Cottage Cheese, 2 cookies (same as Day 3)
Glass of milk

Lunch

Pumpkin Cheese Soup, 10 oz

Snack 2

½ oz walnut
1 tsp honey + cup of tea

Dinner

Buckwheat Porridge, 7 oz (same as Day 3)
Beef chops, 5 oz

Chicken Cutlets

(10 servings)

Ingredients

1 lb 1 ½ oz chicken fillet

1 egg

5 oz carrots

3 ½ oz onion

3 ½ oz whole grain bread

2 tbsp oils

Directions

1. Grind chicken in a food processor.
2. Peel the carrots and onions. Chop them in a food processor.

3. Soak bread in water for 1-2 minutes. Grind bread in a food processor.

4. In a large bowl, mix all the ingredients. Add the egg, salt, and pepper to taste. Stir 5 minutes.

5. Form cutlets or meatballs.

6. Grease the baking sheet with corn or olive oil. Put the cutlets or meatballs on the sheet.

7. Bake for 30-40 minutes at 350 °F. The time depends on the size of the cutlets.

Nutritional facts per serving: 132.5 calories, 14.03g protein, 5.2g fat, 6.43g carbs

Pumpkin Cheese Soup

(4 servings)

Ingredients

1 lb 1 ½ oz pumpkin
10 oz potato
2 L water
2 oz cheese
1/2 cup milk
Salt and pepper to taste
1 oz onions
1 oz leek
1 tbsp vegetable oil

Directions

1. Wash, peel and chop the pumpkin and potatoes into medium cubes.

2. Pour water into the pan. Add the pumpkin and potatoes and bring to boil. Add milk. Cook the vegetables until softened.

3. Peel and coarsely chop the onions and leeks.

4. Preheat oil in a skillet over medium heat. Add the onions and simmer for 5 minutes.

5. Remove the saucepan from the heat. Add the onion to the pot. Beat with a hand blender.

6. Return the pan to the heat. Bring to a boil.

7. Grate the cheese and add to the boiling cream soup. Cook for 5 minutes. Remove the pan from the heat.

Eat your soup with the whole-wheat flour toast. Also, pumpkin seeds or sun-dried tomatoes will be an excellent addition.

Nutritional facts per serving: 185.65 calories, 7.39g protein, 7.9g fat, 24.6g carbs

Beef Chops

(4 servings)

Ingredients

1 3/4 lb beef tenderloin
1 tbsp mustard
1 tsp honey
1 tsp turmeric
2 cloves of garlic
1 tbsp vegetable oil
Salt and spices to taste

Directions

1. Cut the beef into medium portions. Beat them with a kitchen hammer.

2. Combine honey, mustard, turmeric, peeled and crushed garlic, and salt in a bowl.

3. Place the meat in a large bowl. Pour in a mixture of honey and spices. Mix well. Let the meat sit for 1 hour.

4. Grease a baking sheet with oil. Put the meat on the baking sheet.

5. Preheat the oven to 300 °F. Put meat in the oven.

6. Cook the beef for 1 hour.

Nutritional facts: 321 calories, 25.23g protein, 23.28g fat, 3.03 carbs

DAY 5 (1325 calories)

Breakfast
Scrambled Eggs with Zucchini

Snack 1
½ oz walnuts and 2 oz grapes

Lunch
Pumpkin Cheese Soup, 10 ½ oz
Whole grain toast (1 oz) with sun-dried tomatoes (1 oz)

Snack 2
Pumpkin seeds, 1 oz
Mozzarella cheese, 1 oz

Dinner
Boiled Quinoa, 7 oz
Chicken Liver Paste, 7 oz
Fresh tomato, 7 oz

Clean Eating Eggs with Zucchini

(1 serving)

Ingredients

2 eggs
5 oz zucchini
2 oz leeks
Salt to taste
1 tsp corn oil

Directions

1. Wash the zucchini and leek. Thinly slice the vegetables.
2. Heat a non-stick pan over medium heat. Add oil.
3. Add vegetables to the pan. Cook for 5 minutes.
4. Add eggs to the vegetables.
5. Cook for 5-7 minutes.

Nutritional facts: 276 calories, 17.22g proteins, 19.28 fat, 9.37carbs

Boiled Quinoa

(6 servings)

Ingredients

7 oz dry quinoa

800 ml water

Salt to taste

1 tbsp olive oil

Directions

1. Rinse the quinoa thoroughly under running water.

2. Boil water in a small saucepan. Add the Quinoa. Cook for 15 minutes.

3. Add oil and salt to taste.

4. Cook another 5 minutes.

Nutritional facts: 163.52 calories, 56.4g protein, 44.36g fat, 228.2g carbs

Chicken Liver Paste

(6 servings)

Ingredients

1 ½ lb liver
10 ½ oz carrots
2 oz onions
3 ½ oz bacon
Salt and pepper to taste
2 L water
1 tbsp vegetable oil

Directions

1. Pour water into a large saucepan. Add liver, peeled carrots, and bacon.
2. Boil for an hour. Add salt to taste. Boil for another half hour.
3. Remove the saucepan from the heat. Cool.
4. Peel the onion and cut into large cubes. Fry cubes in a frying pan for 5 minutes, stirring.
5. In a food processor, grind all the boiled ingredients and the fried onions.
6. Mix well. Add salt to taste.

Nutritional facts: 264 calories, 27.9g protein, 12.8g fat, 8.9g carbs

DAY 6 (1534 calories)

Breakfast
Cottage Cheese with Raisins, ¾ lb

Snack 1
Grapes, 3 ½ oz

Lunch
Salad with Peach and Celery, 1 lb

Snack 2
1 cup of milk and pita, 2 oz

Dinner
Boiled Quinoa, 7 oz (same as Day 5)
Liver Paste, 7 oz
Fresh cucumber, 3 ½ oz

Cottage Cheese with Raisins

(1 serving)

Ingredients

5 oz cottage cheese
3 ½ oz sour cream
1 banana
1 oz raisins

Directions

1. Place cottage cheese and sour cream in a medium bowl. Add washed raisins.

2. Mix ingredients.

3. Clean the banana and cut it into circles. Put on top of the cottage cheese with sour cream.

A cup of tea perfectly complements this dish.

Nutritional facts: 510 calories, 30.28g protein, 23.8g fat, 43.08g carbs

Salad with Peach and Celery

(1 serving)

Ingredients

3 ½ oz grated celery
3 ½ oz diced peach
3 ½ oz diced bell pepper
3 ½ oz chopped black-eyed peas
2 oz onion half rings
Salt
1 tbsp olive oil

Directions

1. Peel all vegetables and peach and chop.
2. Add ingredients to a medium bowl. Add olive oil and salt. Mix well.

Nutritional facts: 239.3 calories, 6g protein, 10.88g fat, 31.6g carbs

Day 7 (1217 calories)

Breakfast
2 boiled eggs
1 cup of tea
Sun-dried Tomato Toast

Snack 1
Mozzarella cheese, 1 oz
Fresh cucumber, 1 oz

Lunch
Buckwheat and Meatball Soup, 10 ½ oz

Snack 2
Peanuts, ½ oz
Apple, 2 ½ oz

Dinner
Boiled Quinoa, 7 oz (same as Day 5)
Beet and Raisin Salad, 5 oz
Grilled Cod, 7 oz

Sun-dried Tomato Toast

(1 serving)

Ingredients
2 pieces of wholegrain toast
1 oz dried tomatoes

Directions
1. Bread can be toasted in the oven or toaster.
2. Place dried tomatoes on the pieces of toast.

Nutritional facts per serving: 72.6 calories, 2.28g protein, 1.26g fat, 12.9g carbs

Buckwheat and Meatball Soup

(8 servings)

Ingredients

2 oz dry buckwheat
2 ½ L water
2 oz carrot
1 oz onion
7 oz potatoes
7 oz minced chicken
Salt to tast

Directions

1. Pour water into a medium-sized pot. Bring to a boil.

2. Peel the carrots and onions. Cut onions into small cubes and grate the carrots.

3. Place the vegetables in the boiling water.

4. Peel and cut the potatoes into medium-sized cubes. Add to the soup.

5. Make small meatballs from the minced meat. Add to the soup.

6. Wash the buckwheat and add to the soup.

7. Cook the soup for another half an hour.

Nutritional facts per serving: 336 calories, 24.9g protein, 10g fat, 36g carbs

Beetroot and Raisin Salad

(4 servings)

Ingredients
1 lb 2 oz beets
2 oz raisins
3 cloves of garlic
7 oz of natural yogurt
Salt to taste

Directions

1. Boil the beets 90-120 minutes until cooked through in the saucepan.
2. Peel the beets and grate coarsely.
3. Rinse the raisins. Pour boiling water over them and let sit for 15-20 minutes. Drain the liquid.
4. Peel the garlic and chop.
5. In a large bowl, add the beets, raisins, and garlic.
6. Top with yogurt. Add salt to taste. Mix well.

Nutritional facts per serving: 106.78 calories, 28.8g protein, 7.56g fat, 169g carbs

Grilled Cod

(2 servings)

Ingredients

18oz cod

3 tbsp corn flour, for breading

1 tbsp vegetable oil

Salt to taste

Directions

1. Preheat the oven to 350 F.
2. Wash, if necessary, and clean the cod.
3. Grease a baking sheet with oil.
4. Roll the pieces of fish in the flour and place them on the sheet. Salt the fish.

Nutritional facts per serving: 236 calories, 32.56g protein, 5.046g fat, 14.78g carbs

DAY 8 (1244 calories)

Breakfast

Pumpkin Oatmeal Casserole, 7 oz

Sour cream, 7 oz

Snack 1

Walnuts, 0.7 oz

Mozzarella cheese, 1 oz

A cup of tea

Lunch

Beef Soup with Pasta, 300ml

Whole grain bread, 2 oz

Dried tomatoes, 1 ½ oz

Banana, 3 ½ oz

Snack 2

Pita bread, 1 oz

Fresh cucumber, 2 oz

Boiled Chicken, 2 oz

A cup of tea

Dinner

Stewed Chicken with Eggplant and Pepper, 1 lb

Amaranth Porridge, 5 oz

Pumpkin Oatmeal Casserole

(4 servings)

Ingredients

1 lb pumpkin

7 oz cottage cheese

3 1/2 oz yogurt

2 eggs

2 oz oatmeal

1 oz of honey

1 tsp vanilla powder

Directions

1. Wash the pumpkin. Place on a baking sheet. Preheat the oven to 350 °F. Bake for an hour.

2. In a medium-sized bowl, pour oatmeal and add yogurt. Mix well and leave for 2 hours (possibly at night).

3. Peel the pumpkin.

4. Place the pumpkin in a large bowl. Add cottage cheese, soaked oatmeal, eggs, and vanilla. Melt the honey in the microwave. Add honey to the bowl. Beat all ingredients with a food processor.

5. Grease a baking dish with corn oil. Add the casserole mixture.

6. Bake 40 minutes at 350 °F.

Nutritional facts per serving: 167.26 calories, 11.96g protein, 6.86g fat, 16.46 g carbs

Beef Soup with Pasta

(8 servings)

Ingredients

3 ½ oz of potatoes

1 ½ oz carrots

1 oz onion

7 oz of beef

1 ½ oz durum wheat pasta

3 1/2 L of water

Salt to taste

Directions

1. Pour ½ liter of water into the saucepan. Add meat. Bring to a boil. Cook for 10 minutes. Then, remove the pan from the heat. Drain the water. Pour 3 liters of water into the saucepan with meat.

2. Wash and peel the potatoes, onions, and carrots. Cut the onion into small cubes. Finely grate the carrots. Cut the potatoes into medium cubes.

3. Place the carrots and onions in boiling water. Cook for 5 minutes.
4. Add potatoes to the soup. Cook for 30 minutes. Add salt.
5. Add the pasta. Cook for another 10 minutes.

Nutritional facts per serving: 63.38 calories, 4.14g protein, 2g fat, 7.23g carbs

Stewed Chicken with Eggplant and Pepper

(6 servings)

Ingredients

2 lb chicken fillet and leg
1 lb eggplant
10 ½ oz bell pepper
3 ½ oz onion
1/2 L water
1 tbsp honey
1 tsp mustard
1/2 tsp turmeric
1 tsp salt
2 tbsp corn oil

Directions

1. Cut the chicken into pieces. Mix mustard, 1/2 tsp salt, turmeric, and honeyin a small bowl.
2. Place chicken in a large bowl. Add the marinade and mix. Let chicken sit for 3 hours in the refrigerator.
3. Wash and peel vegetables. Cut eggplant, bell peppers and onions into half rings.
4. Preheat the wok pan. Add oil. Add vegetables and 1/2 tsp of salt and simmer for 15 minutes.
5. Place the vegetable in a saucepan w ith a thick bottom. Put meat on top and pour in water. Stew 1 1/2 hours.

Nutritional facts per serving: 146.3 calories, 2.5g protein, 8.3g fat, 15.4g carbs

Amaranth Porridge

(6 servings)

Ingredients

1 cup amaranth
1 small clove of garlic
1 oz onions
3 cups vegetable broth
Sea salt to taste

Directions

1. Peel the onion and garlic. Chop the onion into small cubes and chop the garlic.

2. Mix amaranth, garlic, onions and broth in a 2.5-liter saucepan. Bring to a boil and simmer for about 20-25 minutes, until most of the liquid is absorbed. Mix well. If the resulting mixture is too liquidy or the amaranth is not completely wrinkled (it should be crunchy, but not too hard), boil slightly, stirring continuously, until thickened, about 30 seconds. Add salt.

Nutritional facts per serving: 132.5 calories, 4.8g protein, 2.42g fat, 24.71g carbs

DAY 9 (1299 calories)

Breakfast

Toast with Boiled Egg and Sun-Dried Tomatoes
Toast with Cucumber and Salted Salmon
2 Boiled Eggs

Snack 1

Banana, 3 ½ oz
Walnuts, ½ oz

Lunch

Beef Soup with Pasta, 300ml
Avocado, 2 oz
Whole Grain Bread, 1 ½ oz

Snack 2

Pumpkin Oatmeal Casserole (same as Day 8)
Sour cream, 3 ½ oz

Dinner

Stewed Chicken with Eggplant and Pepper, 1 lb (same as Day 8)
Amaranth Porridge, 5 oz (same as Day 8)

Toast with Boiled Egg and Sun-Dried Tomatoes

(1 serving)

Ingredients

1 oz whole grain bread, toasted
1 boiled egg
1 oz dried tomatoes

Directions

1. Cut the boiled egg into slices. Lay the egg on the toast. Top with dried tomatoes.

Nutritional facts per serving: 171.1 calories, 10.52g protein, 7.63g fat, 14.83g carbs

Toast with Cucumber and Salted Salmon

(1 serving)

Ingredients

1 oz whole grain bread
1 oz salted salmon
1 oz fresh cucumber

Directions

1. Cut cucumber and salmon into slices.
2. Top bread slices with fish and cucumbers.

Nutritional facts per serving: 111.6 calories, 8.44g protein, 4.73g fat, 8.7g carbs

DAY 10 (1226 calories)

Breakfast
Whole grain bread, 1 oz
Salted Salmon, 1 oz
Scrambled Eggs with Zucchini and Pepper

Snack 1
A cup of tea
Roll of Pita Bread and Fresh Cucumber

Lunch
Oatmeal and Meatball Soup, 300ml
Avocado, 2 oz
Whole grain bread, 2 oz
Fresh tomato, 1 ½ oz

Snack 2
Unsweetened yogurt, 150 ml
Banana, 3 ½ oz

Dinner
Corn Pizza with Minced Meat, 7 oz
Beetroot Cheese and Raisin Salad, 7 oz

Scrambled Eggs with Zucchini and Pepper

(1 serving)

Ingredients

2 oz zucchini

1 ½ oz pepper

2 eggs

1 tsp corn oil

Directions

1. Wash and finely chop the zucchini and pepper.
2. Heat the pan. Add oil.
3. Add vegetables to the pan. Cook for 5 minutes.
4. Add eggs to vegetables.
5. Cover the pan and cook for another 5 minutes.

Nutritional facts per serving: 254.13 calories, 15.07g protein, 19.23g fat, 4.57g carbs

Roll of Pita Bread and Fresh Cucumber

(1 serving)

Ingredients

1 oz pita

1 oz fresh cucumber

Directions

Wrap fresh cucumber in pita bread.

Nutritional facts per serving: 51.7 calories, 1.82g protein, 0.23g fat, 10.36g carbs

Oatmeal and Meatball Soup

(6 servings)

Ingredients

7 oz minced chicken

2 oz carrots

1 ½ oz onions

3 ½ oz oatmeal

2 L water

Salt to taste

Directions

1. Pour water into a medium-sized pot. Bring to a boil.

2. Wash and peel the onions and carrots. Grate the carrots. Finely chop the onion.

3. Add the onions and carrots to the boiling water. Cook for 10 minutes.

4. Form minced chicken into balls. Add to the soup. Cook for 10 minutes.

5. Add grain to the soup. Add salt. Cook another 10 minutes.

Nutritional facts per serving: 51.69 calories, 4.89g protein, 2.25g fat, 2.97g carbs

Corn Pizza with Minced Meat

(8 servings)

Ingredients

10 ½ oz cornmeal

1 tbsp dry yeast

2 tbsp honey

2 tbsp corn oil

300ml of water

1 1/3 lb minced chicken

3 ½ oz tomatoes

2 oz Gouda cheese

2 oz sour cream

1 egg

Directions

Dough

1. Heat water. Pour into a large bowl. Pour yeast into water and mix.
2. Add honey and oil to the mixture. Mix until smooth.

3. Pour 150g of cornmeal into the liquid. Knead the dough. Set aside for half an hour.

4. Add flour to the dough and knead.

Pizza

1. Grease a baking sheet with the vegetable oil.

2. Preheat the oven to 350 °F

3. Put the dough on a baking sheet and spread to make the pizza crust.

4. Put the minced meat on the dough. Add salt.

5. Cut the tomatoes into thin slices. Place the slices on the meat.

6. In a small bowl, mix the sour cream and egg. Grease the pizza with the mixture.

7. Place the pizza to the oven. Bake for 40 minutes.

8. Remove pizza from oven. Grate the cheese and sprinkle over the pizza. Return the baking sheet to the oven. Bake another 7-10 minutes.

Nutritional facts per serving: 359.22 calories, 10.1g protein, 15.1g fat, 34.8g carbs

Beetroot Cheese and Raisin Salad

(4 servings)

Ingredients

1lb boiled beets

3 ½ oz Mozzarella cheese

1 ½ oz raisins

7 oz sour cream

2 cloves of garlic

Directions

1. Clean the boiled beets and grate.
2. Rinse the raisins. Add boiling water and leave for 20 minutes. Drain the liquid.
3. Coarsely grate the cheese.
4. Peel and crush the garlic.
5. Mix all ingredients in a big bowl.
6. Add salt and sour cream. Mix well.

Nutritional facts per serving: 100.56 calories, 8.34g protein, 8.96g fat, 22.42g carbs

Day 11 (1421 calories)

Breakfast

Zucchini Omelette, 7 oz

Snack 1

Cottage Cheese with Banana, 7 oz

Lunch

Stuffed Peppers, 10 ½ oz

Beetroot Cheese and Raisin Salad, 7 oz

Snack 2

A cup of milk

Pita Bread, 2 oz

Apple, 3 ½ oz

Dinner

Corn Pizza with Minced Meat, 7 oz (same as Day 10)

Zucchini Omelette

(2 servings)

Ingredients

5 tbsp fat-free cottage cheese
2 eggs + 2 egg whites
7 oz zucchini
salt

Directions

1. Beat cottage cheese with the eggs. Peel the zucchini and finely grate. Mix egg mixture and zucchini and add salt.
2. Place the mixture in a form and bake in the oven at 260 ^{0}F for 25 minutes. Sprinkle with herbs and serve.

Nutritional facts per serving: 191 calories, 17g protein, 9.4g fat, 3.84g carbs

Cottage Cheese with Banana

(1 serving)

Ingredients

3 ½ oz cottage cheese
3 ½ oz banana
1 tbsp yogurt

Directions

1. Place the cottage cheese, banana and yogurt in a medium bowl. Peel the banana, cut into thin circles.
2. Mix the ingredients well.

Nutritional facts per serving: 266 calories, 19g protein, 9.6g fat, 25.04g carbs

Stuffed Peppers

(4 servings)

Ingredients

1 1/3 lb bell pepper, cut into 5 pieces

10 ½ oz chicken fillet

3 ½ oz champignons 3 ½ oz tomatoes

3 ½ oz hard cheese
Salt and spices to taste

Directions

1. Preheat the oven to 350 °F.

2. Cut chicken, tomatoes and mushrooms into small pieces. Grate the cheese.

3. Mix chicken, mushrooms, tomatoes and yogurt for the filling. Salt to taste.

4. Cut the peppers into 2 halves and peel. Leave the stem.

5. Stuff the peppers halves. Put peppers on the baking sheet and place in the oven. Bake for 30 minutes.

6. Remove the dish from the oven. Sprinkle top with cheese and return to the oven to bake for 3-5 min.

Nutritional facts per serving: 222 calories, 27.1g protein, 7.1g fat, 8.9g carbs

Day 12 (1215 calories)

Breakfast
Oatmeal Pancake

Snack 1
Yogurt Dip with Peanut Butter, 1 ½ oz
1 apple

Lunch
Stuffed Peppers, 10 ½ oz (same as Day 11)

Snack 2
Pineapple, 3 ½ oz

Dinner
Baked Turkey, 7 oz
Carrot-Beetroot Salad, 9oz

Oatmeal Pancake

(1 serving)

Ingredients

1 ½ oz oatmeal

1 egg

½ cup milk

1 oz onion

4oz champignons

1 tsp olive oil

2 tbsp parsley

Directions

Filling

1. Pour ½ tsp olive oil into a frying pan.
2. Cut the onion into small cubes and place in the pan. Fry 2 minutes.
3. Add the chopped mushrooms to the onion. Fry for 10–15 minutes.

Pancake

1. Ground oatmeal to a powder.
2. Add egg and milk to the oatmeal. Whisk well.
3. Preheat the pan. Add ½ tsp oil. Pour the batter into a hot pan to make the pancake. Fry for 3 minutes.
4. Flip the oatmeal pancake to cook the other side. Fry for about 1 minute, covering the pan with a lid. Then cover with the other side and cook for another minute.
5. Place the filling on the top of the pancake.

Nutritional facts per serving: 275.9 calories, 17.26g protein, 15.85g fat, 15.37g carbs

Yogurt Dip with Peanut Butter

(4 servings)

Ingredients

1/2 cup Greek yogurt, fat free, plain

1/4 cup natural peanut butter

Directions

In small bowl, combine all the ingredients. Refrigerate for 1 hour.

Nutritional facts per serving: 239 calories, 3.2g protein, 25g fat, 1g carbs

Baked Turkey
(5 servings)

Ingredients
2 lb 3 oz turkey breast
1 cup water
1 tbsp salt
5-6 cloves garlic
pepper mixturc
1 tsp olive oil

Directions

1. Pour salt into a deep cup. Add water and stir. Marinate turkey 2 hours in saltwater in a large bowl. Then remove and dry turkey with a paper towel.

2. Cover the baking sheet with foil and place breast on it. Make cuts in the breast. Stuff the breast with the garlic cloves.

3. In a small bowl, mix oil and pepper. Coat the breast with a mixture.

4. Preheat the oven to 450 °F. Place the pan in the oven for 20 minutes.

5. Turn off the heat. Do not open the oven door for at least 2 hours. Let the breast cool.

Nutritional facts per serving: 149.8 calories, 35.5g protein, 12.8g fat, 1.8g carbs

Carrot-Beetroot Salad

(4 servings)

Ingredients

10 ½ oz beets
7 oz carrots
7 oz potatoes
10 ½ oz pickled cucumbers
1 ½ oz onions
4 tbsp olive oil
Salt to taste

Directions

1. Place the vegetables in a pan. Pour water over vegetables and cook until tender, about 2 hours.

2. Clean the vegetables and cut into medium cubes. Place in a large bowl.

3. Finely chop onions and cucumbers. Add to the bowl.

4. Add the oil. Mix the ingredients.

Nutritional facts per serving: 142.34 calories, 3.7g protein, 7.56g fat, 14.96g carbs

Day 13 (1392 calories)

Breakfast
Carrot-Beetroot Salad, 9 oz (same as Day 12)
Boiled eggs, 2
Whole grain bread, 1 oz

Snack 1
Yogurt Dip with Peanut Butter, 2 oz (same as Day 12)
Pear, 3 oz

Lunch
Baked Turkey, 7 oz (same as Day 12)
Carrot-Beetroot Salad, 9oz (same as Day 12)

Snack 2
Pineapple, 3 ½ oz

Dinner
Asparagus Bean with Egg Batter and Cheese, 7 oz
Boiled Hake, 7 oz

Since the previous day I had prepared enough, for almost the whole day, the issue of food was resolved.

Green Beans with Egg Batter and Cheese

(4 servings)

Ingredients

1.3lb fresh green beans

1.7 oz cheese

2 eggs

2 cloves of garlic

2 liters of water

4 tbsp olive oil

Directions

1. Wash the beans, cut off the ends, and cut the beans into 3-4 pieces.

2. Pour water into a pot and bring to a boil. Add beans pieces to boiling water. Blanch for 3-5 minutes.

3. Drain the liquid.

4. Preheat the pan. Add the oil and green beans. Crush the garlic and add to the pan.

5. Break the eggs into a small bowl and beat with a fork. Pour the eggs into the beans and mix well.

6. Cook for 10 minutes.

7. Coarsely grate the cheese. Add to the beans. Cook for 5-7 minutes, until cheese is melted.

Nutritional facts per serving: 209 calories, 9.4g protein, 16g fat, 5.4 carbs

Day 14 (1602 calories)

Breakfast
Boiled Egg, 2
Salmon Pita

Snack 1
Cottage Cheese, 3 ½ oz
Yogurt, 1 ½ oz

Lunch
Risotto, 2/3 lb
Boiled Chicken Breast 5 oz

Snack 2
Walnuts, 1 oz
Mozzarella, 1 oz

Dinner
Chicken Liver with Apples, 7 oz

Salmon Pita

(1 servings)

Ingredients

1 ½ oz pita
1 oz Iceberg lettuce
1 oz Ricotta cheese
1 oz lightly salted salmon
1 oz cucumber
1 oz shrimp

Directions

1. Place all the ingredients on the pita. Roll it. Refrigerate for 15 minutes.

Nutritional facts per serving: 240.9 calories, 17.33g protein, 6.85g fat, 26.65g carbs

Risotto

(4 servings)

Ingredients

1 oz vegetable oil
2 ½ oz onions
1 clove garlic
5 oz rice
500 ml chicken broth
3 1/2 carrots
9 oz champignons
3 ½ oz bell pepper
1 oz frozen peas
5 oz corn
5 oz tomato

Directions

1. Preheat a deep frying pan over medium heat. Finely chop onion and garlic and add to the frying pan. Cook for 2 minutes. Add rice and cook all ingredients, stirring.

2. Add a little part of broth, 100ml, and boil for 5-7 minutes. Repeat every 5-10 minutes.

3. Add diced carrots, zucchini, and pepper and cook for another 10 minutes, adding to the broth.

4. Add corn, peas, chopped tomatoes, and salt to your risotto. Cook until ready, tender.

5. Put the finished risotto on a plate and top with sprinkle of chopped parsley.

Nutritional facts per serving: 249 calories, 9.77g protein, 6.12g fat, 39.06g carb

Chicken Liver with Apples

(4 servings)

Ingredients

17 ½ oz chicken liver

2 1/2 oz onion

5 oz apple

2 oz yogurt, 1.5%

2 oz water

Salt and pepper to taste

1 tbsp olive oil

Directions

1. Peel and cut the onions. Cut the apples into slices.

1. In a dry non-stick pan, place the onion rings. Cook 3 minutes, until soft.

2. Add coarsely chopped liver to the onion. Mix and stir with a spatula for another 3 minutes.

3. Add sliced apple to the liver and onion.

4. Stew and mix until the liver becomes soft.

5. Add yogurt to the water and pour over the liver-apple-onion mixture.

6. Reduce heat to low and let simmer.

7. Salt and allow to simmer under the lid for about 15 minutes.

Nutritional facts per serving: 218 calories, 23g protein, 10.32g fat, 7.1g carbs

Day 15 (1320 calories)

Breakfast
Eggs in Tomatoes, 10 ½ oz

Snack 1
Salmon Pita (same as Day 14)

Lunch
Lentil Soup, 300 ml
Whole Grain Bread, 1 ½ oz
Boiled Chicken Breast, 5 oz

Snack 2
Walnuts, ½ oz
Honey, 1 tbsp
A cup of tea

Dinner
Baked Chicken with Spinach and Tomatoes

Eggs in Tomatoes

(2 servings)

Ingredients

4 tomatoes, 2/3 lb

4 eggs

green onions to taste

salt, pepper to taste

Directions

1. Preheat the oven to 370 ° F.
2. Cut the caps off the tomatoes. Remove the core and seeds with a spoon.
3. Cover the baking sheet with the parchment.
4. Place hollow tomatoes on a baking sheet.
5. Place an egg into each. Salt to taste.
6. Bake for 25-30 minutes.
7. Pepper to taste. Garnish with green onions.

Nutritional facts per serving: 210.7 calories, 16.06g protein, 12.37g fat, 7.8g carbs

Lentil Soup

(8 servings)

Ingredients

3 ½ oz onions
5 oz carrots
25 oz mushrooms
2 ½ oz olive oil
1 ½ lb cauliflower
9 oz lentils
600 ml water

Directions

1. Peel the carrots, onions, mushrooms. Cut the onions into cubes. Slice the carrots and mushrooms. Preheat the frying pan over medium heat.Fry onions, carrots, and mushrooms in olive oil.

2. Pour the water into the saucepan and bring to a boil. Add the lentils and cook for 10-min.

3. In the other pan boil disassembled into inflorescences cauliflower. Boil for 5min.

4. Place frying onions, mushrooms, carrots, cauliflower to the saucepan. Add lentil to the pot. Mash the ingredients.

5. Add water (600-700 ml) or vegetable milk, boil for 10 min.

Nutritional facts per serving: 221.16 calories, 14.1g protein, 10.35g fat, 20.25g carbs

Baked Chicken with Spinach and Tomatoes

(1 serving)

Ingredients

5 oz chicken fillet

3 ½ oz tomato

1 oz spinach

1 clove garlic

Directions

1. Peel and chop the garlic.
2. Sprinkle the fillet with garlic, salt, and pepper. Sent to the oven until ready (20 min).
3. Tomatoes cut into circles.
4. When the chicken is almost ready - put slices of tomatoes and spinach on the top of the breast.
5. Send the breast for another 2-3 minutes in the oven.

Nutritional facts per serving: 197.32 calories, 36.88g protein, 2.11g fat, 5.5g carbs

Day 16 (1582 calories)

Breakfast
Roasted Veggie Frittata

Snack 1
Cottage Cheese, 5 oz
Yogurt, 3 ½ oz

Lunch
Lentil Soup, 300 ml (same as Day 15)
Whole Grain Bread, 1 ½ oz
Boiled Chicken Breast, 5 oz

Snack 2
Pecan, 1 oz
Mozzarella, 1 oz
A cup of tea

Dinner
Chicken Lettuce Cups, 7 oz

Roasted Veggie Frittata

(6 servings)

Ingredients

3 medium bell peppers
4 garlic cloves
2 large zucchini
1 medium onion
1 tbsp olive oil
¼ cup fresh parsley, chopped
4 eggs
6 egg whites
1 tsp salt
¼ tsp cayenne pepper
1/3 cup finely shredded Parmesan
Nonstick cooking spray

Directions

1. Preheat oven to 420 °F. Place the first oven rack in the lowest position. The second rack must be in the central position in the oven. Line two baking pans with foil. Spray the foil with cooking spray.

2. Place bell pepper and garlic on one pan. Place zucchini and onion on the other baking pan. Brush the products with olive oil. Place zucchini and onion on the center rack and bake 15 minutes. Remove onion and zucchini.

3. Place bell pepper and garlic on the lower rack. Roast for 10 minutes.

4. Peel the bell pepper and garlic. Cut pepper into quarters. Cut the zucchini into three 1/2-inch strips. Cut the onion into ½-inch slices. Chop the parsley. Shred the Parmesan.

5. Place the vegetables and garlic in a bowl. Add parsley and ½ tsp of salt.

6. Lower the heat in the oven to the 330 °F. Coat a 9-x-1.5-inch round cake pan (or smaller) with cooking spray.

7. In a medium bowl, whisk eggs and egg whites. Add remaining salt and cayenne pepper.

8. Add egg mixture to the vegetable mixture. Stir in Parmesan. Place the ingredients into the cake pan.

9. Bake the mixture for 50 minutes.

10. Let the frittata stand 15-30 min before serving.

Nutritional facts per serving: 139 calories, 11g protein, 8g carbs, 7g fat

Chicken Lettuce Cups

(6 servings)

Ingredients

1 ½ tbsp cooking oil

½ chicken breast, pound ground

2 shallots, diced

¼ red onion, diced

1 clove garlic, very finely minced

Fresh chiles, minced, to taste

1 tbsp fish sauce

½ lime, juiced

1 tsp low-sodium soy sauce

1 head iceberg lettuce, leaves separated into cups

1 handful of cilantro

Mint, cut into chiffonade, to taste

Directions

1. Heat a wok over high heat. Alternatively, you can take large sauté pan. Swirl in 1 tbsp oil. Add the chicken. Using a spatula, break up the meat, spreading out over the pan's surface. Cook about 3 minutes, until brown.
2. Add the shallots, onion, garlic, and chiles to the remaining oil in the pan.
3. Place the ground chicken on one side of the pan. Swirl in the garlic-onion mixture. Sauté about 30 seconds, until fragrant.
4. Add the fish sauce, lime juice, and soy sauce to a pan. Cook for 1-2 minutes.
5. Cool the chicken.
6. Serve the chicken in the lettuce cups. Top with the herbs.

Nutrition facts per serving: 120 calories, 6.4g fat, 4.1g carbs, 11.9g protein

Day 17 (1296 calories)

Breakfast
Oatmeal with Apple and Banana, 10 ½ oz

Snack 1
Fruit Salad, 8 oz

Lunch
Carbonara Pasta, 9 oz

Snack 2
Toast (2 oz) with Bean Paste and Cucumber (3 oz)

Dinner
Steamed Hake, 7 oz
Beet and Apple Salad, 7 oz

Oatmeal with Apple and Banana

(3 servings)

Ingredients

7 oz oatmeal flakes
1 banana
½ apples
500 ml of water
1 tsp honey

Directions

1. Boil water.
2. Pour oatmeal in boiling water in a medium bowl. Let it brew for 15 minutes.
3. Add honey to the oatmeal.
4. Peel and cut the banana and apple into slices. Add fruits to the porridge.

Nutritional facts per serving: 301.14 calories, 4.5g protein, 2g fat, 59.25g carbs

Fruit Salad

(2 servings)

Ingredients

2 ½ oz grapefruit
5 oz unsweetened yogurt
2 ½ oz banana
2 ½ oz apple
2 ½ oz kiwi

Directions

1. Peel and cut the fruits into cubes.
2. Take a big bowl, place all the ingredients in it, and mix well.

Nutritional facts per serving: 127.12g calories, 8.61g protein, 4.98g fat, 22.58g carbs

Carbonara Pasta

(3 servings)

Ingredients

7 oz durum wheatpaste
7 oz chicken ham
2 pcs yolk
2 tbsp olive oil
1 ½ oz Parmesan cheese
2 tbsp crushed parsley

Directions

1. Grate the Parmesan cheese using a fine grater.
2. Cut the ham into small slices.
3. Pour boil water into the pan. While it gets a boil, prepare the sauce.

Beat the yolks with a pinch of salt, whisk until light yellow.

4. Add the grated parmesan to the yolks and beat a little.
5. Add chopped parsley leaves (without stems). The sauce is ready.
6. Boil the whole pasta without breaking, for about seven minutes from the moment of boiling, and mix them with slices of ham.
7. Add olive oil and quickly, until cold, pour over the sauce.
8. Stir, cover, and put on low heat.

Nutritional facts per serving: 516.6 calories, 24.6g protein, 24.04g fat, 48.7g carbs

Bean and Pumpkin Seeds Paste

(6 servings)

Ingredients

7 oz beans
5 oz pumpkin seeds
1 oz sesame seeds
2 oz onions
2 oz carrots
2 tbsp cornmeal
Salt and pepper to taste

Directions

1. Rinse the beans. Pour medium saucepan 2 liters of water. Place the beans there. Boil until cooked, add water if necessary.

2. In a dry skillet, fry for 5 minutes pumpkin and sesame seeds. Pour them into a blender cup.

3. Peel the onions, cut into medium cubes, grate the carrots.

4. Pour corn oil (or any other vegetable) into the pan. Place the onions and carrots in it. Stew for 10 minutes stirring.

5. Remove the beans from the water and put in a mixing bowl to the seeds. Also, put the onions and carrots to the blender bowl. Beat ingredients until smooth. You can add bean broth to make the paste softer. Salt.

Nutritional facts per serving: 247.88 calories, 11.31g protein, 16.18g fat, 12.39g carbs

Beet and Apple Salad

(4 servings)

Ingredients

1 lb beets

3 ½ oz apples

2 oz raisins

2 cloves garlic

2 tbsp yogurt

Salt to taste

Directions

1. Boil the beets.
2. Peel the beets and grate them with a coarse grater in a large bowl.
3. Peel the apple from the peel and seeds. Rub on a coarse grater into the same bowl.
4. Rinse the raisins with the boiling water for 15 minutes.
5. Drain the water. Add the raisins to the beet.
6. Add yogurt, salt, and mix the ingredients.

Nutritional facts per serving: 247.88 calories, 2.89g protein, 4.04g fat, 22.9g carbs

Day 18 (1424 calories)

Breakfast

Banana Pancakes with Honey, 3 ½ oz

A glass of milk

Snack 1

Apple Pear Salad, 5 oz

Lunch

Arugula, Cherry and Goat Cheese Salad, 5 oz

Pilaf with Chicken, 9 oz

Snack 2

Cup of tea

Apple-Oat Pie, 3 ½ oz

Dinner

Green Tuna Salad, 7 oz

Boiled Quinoa, 3 ½ oz

Banana Pancakes with Honey

(5 servings)

Ingredients

3 tbsp yogurt
3 tbsp cornflour
3 pcs banana
2 tsp baking powder
1 egg
4 tbsp vegetable oil
½ tbsp sugar

Directions

1. Mix yogurt and egg in a bowl.
2. Mash bananas with a fork in a bowl, add sugar.
3. Mix the flour and baking powder, mix all the ingredients.
4. The consistency of the dough should be as thick as sour cream.
5. Heat the pan, bake pancakes on both sides until golden brown.

Pour the prepared pancakes with liquid honey.

Nutritional facts per serving: 189.06 calories, 3.26g protein, 8.76g fat, 23.96g carbs

Apple Pear Salad

(2 servings)

Ingredients

3 ½ oz apple

3 ½ oz pear

2 oz grapes

2 tbsp yogurt

Directions

1. Wash and peel the apple and pear from the seeds. Cut into small cubes. Place them in a medium bowl. Mix.

2. Wash the grapes. Large grape, you can cut into halves.

3. Add yogurt to the fruits. Mix everything.

Nutritional facts per serving: 75.25 calories, 1.45g protein, 0.8g fat, 16.3g carbs

Arugula, Cherry and Goat Cheese Salad

(2 servings)

Ingredients

2 oz arugula
6 pcs cherry tomatoes
2 oz goat cheese
1 clove garlic
½ tsp wine vinegar
½ tsp salt
½ tsp honey
2 tbsp olive oil

Directions

1. Cut the cherry tomatoes into four parts and fry in olive oil over low heat for 3 minutes.
2. Pass the garlic through a press, add to the pan and fry for another 1 minute.

3. Add salt and sugar to taste. Cook for 1 minute.

4. Place everything to a plate, pour the liquid from the pan into a small bowl.

5. Add vinegar, honey, and one tablespoon of olive oil to the bowl. Mix everything thoroughly.

6. Arugula coarsely tear (you cannot cut at all) and mix with warm cherry tomatoes.

7. Top with goat cheese cut into pieces and pour over everything received refueling.

Nutritional facts per serving: 222 calories, 7.83g protein, 18.5g fat, 5.8g carbs

Pilaf with Chicken

(6 servings)

Ingredients

1 1/3 lb chicken fillet
7 oz rice
5 oz carrots
3oz onion
480 ml water
2 tbsp vegetable oil
½ tsp salt (to taste)

Directions

1. Wash and divide the chicken into parts.

2. Preheat the saucepan over medium heat. Pour oil in it. Place the pieces of the chicken. Fry for 10-15 minutes.

3. Cut the carrots into thin sticks. Onion cut into half rings.

4. Add these vegetables to the meat and fry for another 5 minutes.

5. Pour washed rice, salt and pour water.

6. Gently mix and cook until cooked for 30-40 minutes.

Nutritional facts per serving: 268.9 calories, 25.8g protein, 4.7g fat, 29.4g carbs

Apple-Oat Pie

(6 servings)

Ingredients

3 ½ oz oatmeal
3 ½ oz yogurt
1 ½ oz cornmeal
2 apples
1 egg
1 tbsp honey
1 tbsp corn oil

Directions

1. Pour oatmeal into a medium bowl and pour the yogurt in it, mix. Add corn flour to this mixture, mix. Set aside for 30 minutes.

2. Transfer the mixture to a large bowl, add the egg. Combine.

3. Peel the apples, cut into small cubes. Transfer apples to the oatmeal. Combine.

4. Grease the baking sheet with the oil. Put the dough in the form. Bake at 300 ° F for 40 minutes.

Nutritional facts per serving: 118 calories, 2.77g protein, 4.68g fat, 15.77g carbs

Green Tuna Salad

(8 servings)

Ingredients

2 eggs
6 oz canned tuna
2 tomatoes
1 bell pepper
3 ½ oz lettuce
3 ½ oz arugula
1 tbsp lemon juice
1 ½ oz olive oil
1 tsp salt (to taste)

Directions

1. Boil the eggs.
2. Tomatoes and peppers cut into slices.
3. Wash the lettuce leaves and tear them to a plate.
4. Cut the eggs coarsely, mash tuna with a fork.
5. Stir all the ingredients in a bowl, sprinkle with lemon juice, add olive oil and salt to taste

Nutritional facts per serving: 183.2 calories, 13.22g protein, 12.28g fat, 4.36g carbs

Day 19 (1190.2 calories)

Breakfast

Omelet with Zucchini and Pepper

Snack 1

Chicken Muffins, 1pcs

Lunch

Pilaf with Chicken, 8 ½ oz (as Day 18)

Lettuce Salad, 3 ½ oz

Snack 2

Apple, 1 pcs

Cashew, 1 oz

Dinner

Beets, 3 ½ oz

Beef cutlets, 7 oz

Omelet with Zucchini and Pepper

(1 serving)

Ingredients

2 eggs

50 ml milk

3 ½ oz zucchini

2 oz pepper

1 tsp corn oil

Directions

1. Whisk the eggs in a medium bowl. Add milk and whisk until smooth.
2. Preheat a frying pan over medium heat, pour oil in it.
3. Wash the vegetables and cut them into small cubes.
4. Place the plants in the pan. Stew stirring for 5 minutes.
5. Pour the egg's mixture into the vegetables. Cook for 5-7 minutes.

Nutritional facts per serving: 294.13 calories, 17.42g protein, 21.13g fat, 8.47g carbs

Chicken Muffin

(10 servings)

Ingredients

1 lb chicken fillet
½ cup milk
4 tbsp sour cream
2 eggs
3 ½ oz Parmesan cheese
Spices to taste

Directions

1. Grind the meat with a knife or blender. Send it to a large bowl.
2. Grate cheese coarsely. Add to the meat. Add milk, eggs, sour cream, and spices. Mix well with the spoon.
3. Fill the muffin molds with the mixture. Preheat the oven to 350 °F, place the molds into the oven. Bake for 20 minutes.

Nutritional facts per serving: 140.62 calories, 18.46g protein, 6.39g fat, 0.99g carbs

Beef Cutlets

(6 servings)

Ingredients

10 ½ oz beef

3 ½ oz onion

3 oz whole grain bread

1 egg

Directions

1. Mince the beef, onion, bread using a food processor. Add salt to taste. Combine all ingredients well.
2. Make the balls and press them a little. Take the baking sheet, cover it with the parchment. Place the cutlets on it.
3. Preheat the oven to 350 °F. Bake for 30 minutes.

Nutritional facts per serving: 324 calories, 26.28g protein, 17.34g fat, 15.78g carbs

Day 20 (1609 calories)

Breakfast
Flax Seed Smoothie

Snack 1
Chicken Muffins (same as Day 19), 2 pcs

Lunch
Buckwheat and Meatball Soup, 10 ½ oz (same as Day 7)
Lettuce salad, 3 ½ oz

Snack 2
Carrot and Apple Salad

Dinner
Fresh Cucumber, 3 ½ oz
Beef Cutlets, 5 oz

Flax Seed Smoothie

(1 serving)

Ingredients

3 tbsp flax seeds

2 tbsp pumpkin seeds

3 ½ oz blueberries (fresh or frozen)

3 ½ oz banana

100ml milk

Directions

1. Grind the flax and pumpkin seeds in a coffee grinder.
2. Place the berries in the blender, add ground flax and pumpkin seeds.
3. Pour milk and combine (until smoothie).

Nutritional facts per serving: 474.4 calories, 16.19g protein, 26g fat, 43.81g carb

Carrot and Apple Salad

(2 servings)

Ingredients

5 oz apple

3 ½ oz carrot

3 tbsp sour cream

Directions

1. Wash, peel an apple and carrot. Grate.
2. Put the ingredients in a medium bowl. Add sour cream, mix the ingredients well.

Nutritional facts per servings: 97.5 calories, 2g protein, 5.3g fat, 9.8g carbs

Day 21 (1429 calories)

Breakfast

Zucchini Omelette, 8 oz

Snack 1

Coconut Curd Biscuits, 3 ½ oz

Lunch

Arugula, Cherry and Goat Cheese Salad, 7 oz (same as Day 18)

Boiled Chicken, 7 oz

Snack 2

Pear, 5 oz

Walnuts, ½ oz (or any other nuts)

Dinner

Fresh Cucumber, 3 ½ oz

Beef Cutlets, 5 oz

Zucchini Omelette

(2 servings)

Ingredients

5 tbsp cottage cheese
2 eggs + 2 eggs whites
7 oz zucchini
salt, pepper

Directions

1. Place the cottage cheese in the medium bowl. Add the eggs. Combine the ingredients.
2. Peel the zucchini, grate finely. Add to the cottage cheese mixture.
3. Mix everything, season.
4. Take any mold, pour the mixture in it.
5. Preheat the oven to 260 °F. Place omelet in the oven. Bake for 25 minutes.

Nutritional facts per serving: 191.97 calories, 19.39g protein, 10.6g fat, 4.3g carbs

Coconut Curd Biscuits

(4 servings)

Ingredients

7 oz curd
3 ½ oz coconut chips
3 eggs whites
sweetener to taste
1 tsp water

Directions

1. Combine the curd with the coconut chips in a big bowl.
2. Beat the whites with a food processor until peaks. Add sweetener and water.
3. Mix two masses and form the cookies of the desired size.
4. Preheat the oven to 390 ° F. Bake cookies for about 30-35 minutes until golden brown.

Nutritional facts per servings: 148 calories, 14.6g protein, 10.1g fat, 3.6g carbs

Baked Chicken with Broccoli

(2 serving)

Ingredients

7 oz chicken breast

7 oz cauliflower or broccoli

½ cup milk

1 egg

Directions

1. Preheat the oven to 350 ° F.
2. Cut the baked chicken fillet into medium cubes.
3. Take a big baking sheet. Place the chicken on it. Add boiled broccoli on top.
4. Pour the sauce on the top of the dish.
5. Add salt and pepper to taste.
6. Pace the sheet into the oven. Cook for 10 min.

Sauce

1. Pour milk into the bowl. Add the egg. Beat the ingredients.

Nutritional facts per serving: 416 calories, 31.69g protein, 7.1g fat, 8.1g carbs

Thank you for spending three weeks with me. I hope that it was tasty, and you have a new habit of healthy eating. Leave your feedback and suggestions, because we want to become better with you.

Karla Bro

Made in the USA
Columbia, SC
08 March 2023

13517902R00081